PREFACE

by Nury Vittachi

TWO GODS were sitting around drawing up the rules of the universe, the formulas of time and space, the laws of physics and so on. "Well, that's gravity done. What else do we have to do?" asked one.

"I reckon the principles of economics could do with a bit more examination," the other replied. "I'm not convinced that they'll actually work in practice."

"There's only one way to find out," said the first god. "Let's try 'em out."

So they chose an obscure corner of the world and built a city designed to take to extremes all the principles of free market capitalism, the enterprise economy and laissez-faire government.

The result was Hong Kong, a bizarre society where my tea-lady wears a gold watch and owns a flat which is worth more than its equivalent in Park Avenue, New York.

Okay, I'm not saying that this version of Hong Kong's origins will be backed up by archival documents concerning a certain Captain Charles Elliot, who landed on the island of Heung Gong in 1841. But looking at the territory from this point of view has helped me understand this wild and crazy city. In many ways, Hong Kong is not a place at all. It is an economic experiment in concrete form, a chapter which has fallen out of one of Adam Smith's economics books and taken flesh.

This is not to say that Hong Kong has found the key to the perfect society: not at all. The road from insolvent colony to rich territory has been long and painful and there is still pain to come, as the community strives to create as happy a relationship with its new sovereign as it has had with its present one.

The territory has long been a role model for its neighbours — but not an easy one to emulate. A unique set of physical, sociological, political and economic factors has made it what it is. But if the model cannot be replicated, it can at least be learned from.

The coastal territory is modern and futuristic, yet also superstitious and traditional. It is Eastern and it is Western. It is very cosmopolitan and it is very Chinese.

All the different faces of Hong Kong are captured in this marvellous book, which freezes the action at a dramatic point in its history: at the time of handover, as a British colony becomes a Chinese special region.

There are many books of photographs of Hong Kong on the market, but the *Over Hong Kong* series has always been held far and away the most popular.

There is a simple reason for this. You'll find no false artistry in here, no colour filters, no manipulative attempts to put a positive face on the images. With its glittering towers and smoky factories, with its grimy boatyards and lush countryside, the city state is left to speak for itself.

OVER HONG KONG

Photographs by Magnus Bartlett and Kasyan Bartlett

Introduction by David Dodwell

Preface by Nury Vittachi

Pacific Century Publishers Limited

OVER HONG KONG Volume Four
THIRD EDITION

Pacific Century Publishers Ltd 1996
© Airphoto International Ltd

ISBN 9622174639

Satellite image of Hong Kong
Spot Asia Pte Ltd © CNES 1996

All enquires to:
Pacific Century Publishers Ltd
1003 Kowloon Centre
29-43 Ashley Road, Kowloon, Hong Kong
Tel: 2376 2085 Fax: 2376 2137
E. mail: airman@gateway.net.hk

Colour separation by K. Graphics
Printing by Midas Printing Ltd
Production supervision by Twin Age Ltd
Captions by Peter Fry and Hilary Binks
Designed by George Ngan

Printed in Hong Kong

CONTENTS

▌Facing title page
Hong Kong Clearly showing Chek Lap Kok at lower left, the "old" airport, Kai Tak is to the right of Kowloon Peninsula. The top of this satellite Image (Spot Asia Pte Ltd ©CNES) reveals the intensity of development in adjacent Shenzhen.

▌Preceding page
Wanchai Nowhere on Hong Kong Island has changed more dramatically over the past decade than Wanchai. The former down-market district has sprouted gleaming high-rise shopping malls, hotels and office complexes, including one of Asia's tallest buildings, the 78-storey Central Plaza (right). Soon Wanchai will boast Hong Kong's newest landmark, the extension to the Hong Kong Convention & Exhibition Centre, scheduled for completion in mid-1997.

▌Right
Po Lin Monastery The sun sets on the golden roofs of Po Lin Monastery, located among the western mountains of Lantau Island and symbolically blessed by the Temple of Heaven Buddha. In 1278 the last boy emperor of the failing Song Dynasty fled to lonely Lantau in a desperate attempt to escape his enemies. Today Lantau embodies not only Hong Kong as it once was, but the territory's future, with the advent of the world's largest infrastructure project: the Port and Airport Development Scheme.

INTRODUCTION

by David Dodwell

Hong Kong is a paradox. Maybe even a contradiction in terms. So many people ought not to be able to live in such a handful of square miles. So few people ought not to have been able to build the world's eighth largest trading power. They ought not to have savoured such stability during a century of almost unprecedented chaos just a dozen miles to their north. So wealthy a place ought not to be home to so many pockets of poverty.

"Over Hong Kong" is a tribute to this paradox: a story of men's ability to bend nature to meet their needs, but at the same time a tribute to the awesome resilience of nature.

It also raises troubling questions about just how much the territory's long-suffering environment can take, as migrants from mainland China continue to pour through Shenzhen to seek their fortunes in the territory, as port planners talk of needing five times more port capacity by 2020 than exists today if Hong Kong is to retain its pole position as a hub for international trade, and as a substantial proportion of the world's dredger fleet is already at work in Hong Kong waters reclaiming literally thousands of hectares of land from the sea.

At the heart of this reclamation is of course Hong Kong's new airport at Chek Lap Kok, and the hundreds of projects associated with it - from the dramatic Tsing Yi bridge, to the massive reclamation along Kowloon's western shore, to the latest stride northward of Hong Kong Island's northern shore - all of them graphically portrayed in the pages ahead.

There is much angst about the plight of northern Lantau as the new airport nears completion, preparing for aircraft to begin touching down early in 1998. Already, the mountain island of Chek Lap Kok has been flattened and consigned to history. Still more land will be carved from the sea if plans go ahead for a new container port on north Lantau. The Chinese white dolphin which frequents these waters, and whose world has been thrown awry by such unprecedented marine turbulence, may also soon be part of history if gloomy environmental groups are to be believed.

But there is a more positive side to the Chek Lap Kok story. It will liberate for the first time in half a century the 27,500 long-suffering Kowloon residents living in the flight path to Kai Tak - liberate them from noise levels that most normal humans would not tolerate as 400 aircraft lumber overhead every day: liberate them from the indignity of having aircraft passengers passing so close that from their porthole windows they can virtually tell what kind of soup a family happens to be serving for supper: liberate them from a blight on development that has left apartment blocks in the area among the most disgracefully dilapidated in Hong Kong.

And as those articles from the venerable Far Eastern Economic Review remind us (at left), Kai Tak was already full to brimming in 1947. If the planners of her Imperial government and Royal Air Force engineers had had their way, Hong Kong would have had a new airport in operation in Deep Bay by early 1949 - costing the grand sum of £4m.

HONG KONG'S NEW AIRFIELD

The necessity and urgency of a new airfield has been recognised by all commercial airlines, the travelling public and government. The facilities of Kai Tak have been considered inadequate many years before the war primarily on account of the hillside to the north of the field, and secondly because of relatively short runways.

Construction will require several engineering feats such as the dynamiting of four million cubic yards of granite which will be used for reclamation of the western shore of Deep Bay. Until the completion of this field Kaitak will have to serve the needs of Hong Kong.

FAR EASTERN ECONOMIC REVIEW. 1947

▮ Left
Hong Kong, 1980s Hong Kong in the mid-1980s featured a Kowloon considerably smaller than it has now become. At upper left, the container port extends only to Terminal Six, and Stonecutters Island is just that: an island. Kowloon extends into the harbour as it has since land reclamation created Tsim Sha Tsui East in the sixties, with the familiar Yaumatei Typhoon Shelter flanking its western side. The Eastern Harbour Crossing tunnel is being completed: its Quarry Bay entrance can be seen at lower right. Note that this view encompasses both of the horse racing tracks, at Happy Valley and at Sha Tin.

Kowloon City The familiar two-runway International Airport here appears from along the pilot's approach path, right over hundreds of thousands of people. Aircraft actually come in much lower over the buildings below; in 1995, the airport authorities even temporarily halted flights landing or taking off from this direction. Its official two runways simply designate the two possible approaches, from the west northwest, and the east southeast. Kai Tak is truly a one-runway international air nexus serving the entire globe.

Right
Kai Tak International Airport A Cathay Pacific aircraft in its new livery, introduced in 1994, arrives in Hong Kong, while a Polar Air Cargo plane heads for the freight terminal. This, basically, is the entire Kai Tak airport, minus its support facilities. In 1948, government officials debated moving the 'Kaitak Aerodrome' to another site, and finally decided on Deep Bay. In 1998, fifty years later, Kai Tak will finally become history.

Right
Kai Tak International Airport Kai Tak does not look all that crowded from this perspective. But that is only because it has continually expanded its tarmac for parking planes, as well as enlarging its terminal. Authorities have constructed two tarmac expansions since the early '80s, seen here to the left of the original, which is adjacent to the terminal building at right. The final expansion consists of an apron extending parallel to the runway itself.

What then would have been the plight of the Mai Po marshes (page 110), which continue today to play precarious host to thousands of migrating birds, or of the rural backwaters in the north western New Territories between Yuen Long and Tuen Mun (page 108).

We must suppose the Chinese revolution in 1949 put paid to plans to build an airport so close to China's border, but it is yet further evidence of the paradoxical quality of Hong Kong that Kai Tak, an airport already condemned as inadequate and overcrowded in 1947, should almost 50 years later still be serving Hong Kong's needs successfully as the world's fourth busiest international airport. There is a lesson somewhere here about necessity and invention.

In some respects, Hong Kong's environment is fortunate. That may sound heretical, but it is not. Hong Kong has suffered almost no harm at the hands of heavy industry. Many of its steep granite slopes are so inhospitably steep that they have kept even the most sophisticated developers at bay, leaving pristine pockets even in the most urban areas of the territory which provide home for animals and plants which could normally never subsist so cheek by jowl with people. Landslides frequently triggered by summer's monsoon rains are also a constant reminder of nature's power, and the precarious hold men have gained over the land.

It is also not insignificant that the transfer over the past two decades of much of Hong Kong's manufacturing industry into the mainland of China has reduced the pressure from industrial pollution. As a services economy has emerged to take the place of manufacturing, so many pollutive pressures have been relieved.

Compare Hong Kong's environmental troubles with those of the smokestack cities of Shenyang, Benxi, Fushun and Anshan, up in north eastern China - which are no longer visible in satellite photographs for many months of the year because of the stinging orange haze that hangs over their steel, coal and heavy engineering plants. These factories throw into the atmosphere around 15 million tonnes of sulphur dioxide every year, creating a 1,600 kilometre smoke trail out over the Pacific Ocean that blights large parts of Japan with acid rain.

China's environmental authorities say 86 per cent of the country's rivers passing through cities are seriously polluted - partly because of the 600 million tonnes of solid industrial waste created by its factories every year. Authorities in nearby Guangzhou get 10,000 calls a year from residents alarmed by nearby pollution.

From this frightful perspective, Hong Kong is indisputably fortunate - but still the city is rated among the least liveable-in in the world. The US magazine *International Living* put Hong Kong bottom of a list of 192 territories when it drew up its 1995 Quality of Life Index. However one argues about the appropriateness of the factors used to assemble such an index, there is little disputing that even as manufacturing industry has migrated, the territory remains under pressure from two principal directions: population, and trade. Each has already taken a terrible toll, and pressures are likely to get worse rather than better. But at the same time, it is population and trade that provide Hong Kong's lifeblood. This is a Catch 22 that cannot easily be resolved.

Hong Kong's steep mountain slopes have squeezed the population into urban high-rise canyons where voyeurs can thrive as much on the sixtieth floor as on the second. Population pressures are by far the most acute in the world: the United Nations says more than twice as many people are squeezed into the city as are squeezed into the world's second most congested city, Lagos.

High-rise housing estates, gouged mountainsides, and reclamation are only the most visible signs of population

Right
Chek Lap Kok, 1990 In 1990, Chek Lap Kok looked like this, pristine and seemingly utterly isolated from the modern age. The island, unpopulated, was home to the very rare Romer's Frog and thickets of mangroves, and featured bare rocky hillsides on its northern end. Tung Chung New Town will soon replace the villages at right, eventually housing 200,000 residents. Chek Lap Kok first gained attention in 1810: a famous sea battle between the allied forces of Chinese imperial, British naval and Macanese warships, and the famed pirate Cheung Po Tsai took place here. Cheung escaped the trap.

pressure. The territory faces serious marine pollution, as the great majority of Hong Kong's sewage continues to flow untreated into the sea. The little orange garbage gatherers which bob around Victoria Harbour scoop a total of 17 tonnes of floating flotsam every day. A total of 2m cubic metres of heavily polluted waste water - equivalent to about 1,000 Olympic-sized swimming pools - is discharged into the harbour and coastal waters every day by more than 21,000 major polluters. This inevitably poisons fish stocks and has inflicted perhaps terminal damage on the territory's once-thriving oyster-breeding industry (page 105). Only by the end of 1997 does the government expect to staunch sewage flows into Victoria Harbour.

Then there is air pollution. Unleaded fuel became available in the territory only in 1991. While most private cars have by now been converted to unleaded fuel, highly pollutive diesel engines continue to power most of the territory's taxis and heavy goods vehicles.

But it is not simply burgeoning population that is creating these strains. The territory's hectic growth as an entrepot for China has forced the government to expand port facilities at breakneck speed. Hong Kong's container port remains the busiest in the world, handling more than 12 million containers last year, most of them being transported directly by train, road or river boats from cities in the Pearl River delta. New container berths are being added as fast as they can be built, and still a significant share of containers have to be loaded and unloaded in mid-harbour by thousands of inelegant, but highly efficient lighters. The sight of this commerce - quite literally the lifeblood of Hong Kong's economy - is breathtaking - and captured in all its drama in the pages ahead, from the thickets of tower cranes at Kwai Chung (page 94-97) to the queues of container ships travelling towards Victoria Harbour down the Lamma channel (page 66).

But inevitably, the hectic growth of this commerce is creating myriad strains - not least a sense of massive maritime traffic congestion throughout Hong Kong's narrowing harbour (page 36). Where the rural spaces in other countries find themselves littered with illicit garbage dumps, Hong Kong finds empty containers littering nooks and crannies in the quiet spaces in the Kwai Chung hinterland (page 103). Clearly, such pollution is superficial - doubly so when one sees how speedily a bus abandoned on a roadside can be overrun by Hong Kong's tropical flora - but one has to wonder whether there is a lesson in reports from the United States of old army tanks being dumped in the ocean to provide "ideal" habitats for marine life.

Hong Kong people don't need to count the abandoned containers to know the territory is under strain. But the reluctance of Hong Kong's unintrusive government to gather all but the most essential statistics may make things seem worse than they really are. As it looks at comparative environmental data, the World Economic Forum's annual World Competitiveness Report ranks Hong Kong at the bottom of 48 countries surveyed - not because pollution is known to be comparatively awful, but simply because data is not available.

One set of available data would have us believe that Hong Kong should already be well on top of its environmental problems. According to economists at the World Bank, rising living standards are supposed to help the environment. The theory goes that wealthier families want fewer children, which in turn reduces population pressures. The theory also says that as families become wealthier so they shift attention from the subsistence priorities of food, education, health and welfare spending, and pour more cash into quality of life areas - like improving the environment.

Left
The Harbour, 1995 In this view, in which Sha Tin and Tolo Harbour recede into the distance, reclamation relentlessly crowds in on the harbour. The reclamation on Kowloon-side is essentially complete, except for filling in the gap between the reclaimed land and the existing peninsula. It will expand the Kowloon's area by one-third. But on Hong Kong's north side, work has just begun. The two extensions already reclaimed indicate the outline of the final expansion, which will extend from Central to Causeway Bay.

Left and Above
West Kowloon Reclamation The Western
Harbour Crossing emerges at its northern terminus, as
construction proceeds on the West Kowloon
Reclamation's southern end. The Crossing actually consists
of two separate tunnels. Three lanes in each direction,
unprecedented in Hong Kong's extensive history of
building tunnels, will carry vehicular traffic towards the
western side of Hong Kong Island, at Sai Ying Pun; the rail
tunnel will convey express trains between Central and the
airport in 23 minutes. In the view at left, the rail tunnel
entrance appears to the right of the road tunnel.

Above
The West Kowloon Expressway Running alongside Kwai Chung Road, the new West Kowloon Expressway will not only connect Hong Kong Island with the new airport, but also with Route 3 to China via a new bridge between Tsing Yi and the New Territories. Adjacent to the open parkland by the new highway is the Lai Chi Kok district. Stonecutters Island is at upper right, and the container port at Kwai Chung at right.

The World Bank would have us believe that the turning point comes when gross domestic product per capita passes US$4,000 a year. But Hong Kong's GDP per capita has run past US$24,000, and it is far from clear that any turning point has been reached. Rather than contradict World Bank economists, it is arguable that special circumstances in Hong Kong account for so massive a discrepancy.

First, it would be unfair to suggest that Hong Kong has seen no benefits as average wealth has risen. Local families are indeed having fewer children, and government spending on environmental problems has begun to rise strongly, reaching almost HK$5 billion in 1994. A total of HK$8.1bn is budgeted for dealing just with sewage in Victoria Harbour. Pollution will be cut by 70 per cent when work is complete in 1997.

South east Asia's first chemical waste treatment facility was commissioned in Hong Kong in 1994, treating 100,000 tonnes a year - suggesting that Hong Kong is not a laggard, but simply that the scale of the task of dealing with waste in such a congested area is quite literally overwhelming. It may be a tribute to the effectiveness of

Above
Tsing Ma Bridge With the lifting into position of
the final bridge deck units of the Tsing Ma and Kap Shui
Mun Bridges in March 1996, Lantau Island was finally
joined to Kowloon for the first time. Completion of the
deck erection represents a major milestone in the
construction of the Lantau Fixed Crossing connecting the
new airport at Chek Lap Kok with urban Hong Kong.

programmes in place that *Over Hong Kong* shows no ready evidence of how or where the territory's 20,000 tonnes of municipal waste is disposed of every day.

In addition, the territory has an honourable record when it comes to recycling waste. While in the US and Britain less than one third of waste paper is recycled, in Hong Kong almost two thirds is recycled. When it comes to plastics, Hong Kong recycles over 40 per cent, while just 7 per cent is recycled in Britain, and a mere 3 per cent in the US. Similar discrepancies exist in recycling ferrous and non-ferrous metals - where over four fifths is recycled in Hong Kong.

But Hong Kong's special circumstances have dulled the reflexes that economists appear to have taken for granted when they forecast that governments would begin to get on top of environmental problems by the time average wealth passed US$4,000 a head. First, they could not have taken account of the steady flow of immigrants into the territory from the mainland of China. The official flow is 150 per day, but this takes no account of illicit

Hong Kong, Kowloon and Lantau Looking from south of Tai Lam Country Park, two new bridges will soon span once uncrossed distances: the Tsing Ma suspension bridge connecting Tsing Yi Island with Ma Wan, and the cable-stayed Kap Shui Mun bridge from Ma Wan to Lantau Island. The Tsing Ma bridge, at 2.2 kilometres, will be the world's longest combined rail and road suspension bridge. The bridges will connect with the North Lantau expressway, and will have three lanes in each direction. Underneath, trains will travel at 135 kilometres per hour, much faster than the 80 kilometres which the Mass Transit Railway now achieves. This perspective spans Hong Kong's skyline from Tsuen Wan at far left to Kowloon and Hong Kong Island, with Pok Fu Lam and the Wah Fu Estates at its western end.

Tsing Ma Bridge The view above towards Ma Wan Island suggests how contractors constructed the bridge towers: step by step, and section by section. By April 1994, the 500 tonne saddles had been placed atop each tower, and the job of turning 160,000 kilometres of wire into two 15,000 tonne cables began, not in a factory, but in position, using a special pulley which ran back and forth between the two towers. This process is called 'cable spinning'; in this case enough wire was used to circle the earth four times. Technicians then compacted, wrapped and painted the cables.

arrivals, nor of visitors who overstay on short-stay visas. This influx makes a nonsense of what would otherwise be Hong Kong's declining population trend, and one must assume that as the territory reverts to Chinese sovereignty in 1997, so the influx will rise rather than fall.

If the first distorting influence is immigration, then the second is likely to be emigration. A significant proportion of the territory's middle classes - who account for most of the taxpayers - have no intention of staying in Hong Kong through into retirement. They have been busy in recent years acquiring foreign passports, putting their children into schools in Canada, Australia, the United States and elsewhere, and finding attractive homes nearby. Many have clear priorities to earn and save as much as possible while they live in Hong Kong, and to keep their tax liabilities to a minimum. It is open to question whether they will be enthusiastic financiers of any ambitious environmental clean-up in Hong Kong when their own long-term interest is likely to be in the environment of Vancouver or Sydney or Melbourne.

Such a view may be unduly pessimistic or cynical. After all, for every middle class Hong Kong professional that has laid plans to emigrate, there must be two that have no intention of going anywhere. It is also a very short-sighted family that resigns itself to a working lifetime of pollution and squalor in the quest for comfort in their twilight years.

For whatever reasons, Hong Kong taxpayers remain comparatively reluctant to give a high priority to cleaning up the environment. But changing circumstances across the China border may force urgent changes in the not too distant future. Economic developments in the Pearl River delta region are quite literally muddying the waters as far as Hong Kong's environmental priorities are concerned.

This area of 66 million people and more than 100 towns and cities has been growing at a rate of 14 per cent a year since the Chinese economy began opening up to the outside world in 1979. In 1994, growth passed 18 per cent. The area is now home to at least 55,000 Hong Kong-funded joint ventures. Hong Kong's polluting companies - whether in textiles, bleaching and dyeing, the manufacture of printed circuit boards, electroplating, or food processing - may have moved out of Hong Kong, but many have not moved very far. While once their pollution spilled directly into Hong Kong Harbour, today it spills into the tributaries of the Pearl River, and into the Guangdong watertable. It is clear that as the region continues to industrialise, so it is only a matter of time before Hong Kong feels its pollutive grip. Questions are already being asked about the quality of Hong Kong's water supply, most of which is piped from Dongguan county immediately to the north of Shenzhen.

Questions will only intensify as the Guangdong authorities press ahead with their plans to draw heavy industry into the area. Nor has anyone begun to factor the likely effect of 20 airports operating in the Pearl River delta, and almost 100 new ports along the Guangdong coast. As more power stations are built, so they are likely to be fuelled not by clean imported Australian coal as in Hong Kong, but by sulphur-rich Chinese stocks - gifting Hong Kong with acid rain that it has so far lived without.

All this is occurring at a time when the emergence of Hong Kong as a services economy rather than a manufacturing centre is likely to bring relief from industrial pollution. Within a few years, the pollutive threat may be less from within than from across the border with China - which suggests that the environmental awareness of people in cities like Foshan, Shunde, or even bristling Shenzhen leaning across Hong Kong's land border within

Lantau Fixed Crossing The 3.5-kilometre Lantau
Fixed Crossing, comprising the 1,377-metre Tsing Ma
Bridge connecting Tsing Yi and Ma Wan, the viaduct over
Ma Wan, and the 820-metre Kap Shui Mun Bridge
between Ma Wan and Lantau, is well on target for
completion by mid-1997. The Kap Shui Mun Bridge links
with the beginning of the 12.5 kilometre, three-lane North
Lantau Expressway along the north coast of Lantau,
leading to Chek Lap Kok Airport and Tung Chung New
Town. The Tsing Ma Bridge deck is 62 metres above sea
level, enabling ocean-going ships to continue to use the
Rambler Channel (above). In the foreground, another new
bridge will link Tsing Yi with Ting Kau in the northwest
New Territories.

shouting distance of the immaculate greens of the Fanling golf course (page 112), may in due course play a bigger part in determining Hong Kong's environmental fate than awareness in Hong Kong itself. That is not very good news if the World Bank's economists really are right about the US$4,000 GDP per capita threshold for rising concern over the environment, because average incomes across the Pearl River delta still languish well short of this.

It is easy to become gloomy. *Over Hong Kong* provides ready evidence of the environmental strains bearing down on the territory. But at the same time it provides stunning evidence of the dramatic beauty - both urban and rural - that is still visible across Hong Kong. The long views across Hong Kong's mountain ridges, or across Sharp Peak in Saikung (page 122-125) are a reminder that 40 per cent of Hong Kong's land area remains country park.

Perhaps most evocative of all is the 34-metre high Temple of Heaven Buddha facing north from high above Lantau's Po Lin monastery (page 156-7). As the Buddha looks calmly over to Chek Lap Kok, and on towards the Chinese mainland, one has to wonder whether its raised right hand is held up in supplication, or in tranquil confidence that ultimately man and nature can find in Hong Kong some kind of tolerable equilibrium. *Over Hong Kong* has no way of providing an answer, but it presents a unequalled portrait of what could be lost if no equilibrium is found.

■ Above
Chek Lap Kok and Tung Chung New Town
The 1,248-hectare airport platform at Chek Lap Kok, north Lantau, was completed in June 1995 after 31 months of reclamation and excavation. The airport is scheduled to open with the first of its 3,800-metre-long runways in April 1998. Capable of operating 24 hours a day, it will be able to handle 35 million passengers and 3 million tonnes of air cargo annually. Airport facilities have been designed with future expansion in mind: ultimately Chek Lap Kok will serve 87 million passengers and handle 9 million tonnes of cargo a year. A further 67 hectares of land have been reclaimed along the north shore of Lantau for Phase 1 of Tung Chung New Town, which will house 200,000 people by 2011 and will provide a supporting community for the new airport.

THE ISLAND

Preceding page
Hong Kong Island Looking eastwards from above Victoria Peak, it is clear how development is concentrated along the north shore (left) and, to a lesser extent, the south shore (right), while much of the island remains virgin territory.

Above
Central, 1983 'Betsy', the original DC-3 aircraft purchased by Cathay Pacific Airways in 1946, returned home to Hong Kong in March 1983. In the background can be seen Central as it then was: including The Bank of America, the Far East Finance Centre, Admiralty, and the then-named Connaught Centre with its round windows. Note that in this view, Government House is clearly visible behind the Furama Hotel.

Right
Central, 1994 Essentially the same view as opposite, but the years have seen numerous changes. The many banks in the business district appear, appropriately enough, to fall under the shadow of I.M. Pei's mirrored masterpiece, the Bank of China Tower. Among them: The Hongkong Bank, the Standard Chartered Bank, the Bank of America and Citicorp. As for Central's hotels, the Hilton has closed, but the squarish Mandarin Oriental at right and the Furama Kempinski with its revolving restaurant atop it remain, the latter with a new neighbour, the Ritz Carlton. Government House is no longer visible from the harbour, and the old Tamar Naval Basin at left has since been filled in for redevelopment.

Preceding pages
Hong Kong Island From atop the Peninsula's new tower, Hong Kong scintillates with absolutely unsurpassed beauty. Following the waterfront from east to west, the golden sides of Asia's tallest building, Central Plaza, probably should win top awards for lighting design. To the left of the NEC neon, three logos identify the hotels at Pacific Place: yellow for the Island Shangri-La, red for the Conrad and the J. W. Marriott to its left. Next to the yellow and green-lit Hongkong Bank building, the apparent steps of the Standard Chartered Bank's headquarters cast a strange glow. While the round Jardine House windows appear normally lit, the Exchange Square buildings have also chosen green for their night-time image. The building, green once more, between the two pillars houses government offices. Further down the waterfront, the '999' advertisement sits just before the Shun Tak Centre on the side of a multi-storey carpark.

Right
Western Shun Tak Centre, the two black and red-striped buildings fronted by the Macau Ferry Terminal at centre, for its first ten years housed the Hotel Victoria in its east tower. In 1995 Hotel Victoria closed, not due to poor occupancy rates but simply because its owners could make more money converting it into a commercial and office building. The whole of Western, stretching out behind Shun Tak, will likely become an increasingly important business district. This seems particularly apt, as it was here that the British first landed in 1841, at Possession Point. That geographic feature, however, long ago disappeared amidst earlier land reclamations.

Far right
Central The gardens of Government House (centre), the Hong Kong Botanical Gardens (front) and Hong Kong Park (right) form a vital green oasis in the heart of Central business district. When Government House was constructed in 1855-6, it enjoyed an uninterrupted view across Victoria Harbour to Kowloon. Originally a square neo-classical building, it has been considerably altered since, most notably by the addition of a quasi-Oriental tower by the Japanese during the Second World War. Today Government House is hemmed in by futuristic towers of high finance, as the territory's major banks cluster together. Beyond Hong Kong Park, which occupies the site of the old Victoria Barracks, is the Pacific Place shopping/office/hotel complex.

Left

Central Marching along the waterfront like soldiers in Hong Kong's continual march towards an ever more prosperous future, these buildings form the core of Hong Kong's Central business district. Oddly enough, the one truly military structure, The Prince of Wales Building at far left, is the most anachronistic. It will soon be torn down and the site rebuilt by the Chinese-backed company CITIC Pacific, which in 1995 out-bid other rivals in one of Hong Kong's carefully watched property auctions. The new reclamation along the island's northern waterfront will provide yet more investment opportunities for Chinese companies hungry to enter the local market.

Above

Tsim Sha Tsui and Hong Kong Island The tip of Kowloon peninsula known as Tsim Sha Tsui, with its distinctive architectural styles, provides a visual counterpoint to the ever changing business district on the north side of Hong Kong Island. Until fairly recently, this portion of Hong Kong Island was designated the City of Victoria, a name which appears even today in some atlases as the territory's 'capital', quite distinct from the city of Kowloon. But Hong Kong-side expands eastwards and westwards without regard to boundaries, and indeed literally towards Kowloon as well: the reclamation at far left will expand the Hong Kong Convention and Exhibition Centre. The reclamation at Sai Ying Pun rounds the corner on the island's right side, with Green Island behind.

The Harbour Hong Kong and Kowloon reach out
to each other, closing in on either side of the original
harbour, once considered the colony's most valued asset.
The West Kowloon Reclamation extends at right, a major
component of the Port and Airport Development Scheme
which will connect Hong Kong Island to the mainland with
yet *two* more tunnels: one rail and one vehicular. The island
status of Kellet Island, sunlit at bottom, ended with the
advent of the first Cross-Harbour Tunnel, nearly a quarter
century ago. Nonetheless, the Royal Hong Kong Yacht
Club still flourishes on this prime location.

Hong Kong Convention & Exhibition Centre
Built on reclaimed land jutting dramatically into Victoria
Harbour from the Wanchai waterfront, the new HK$4.8
billion extension to the Hong Kong Convention &
Exhibition Centre occupies a prime location unrivalled by
any other convention facility in the world. The new
extension will more than double the Centre's existing
space: at a total of 250,000 square metres in floor area,
the Centre will rank as one of the biggest in Asia.

Left
Wanchai Waterfront The Hong Kong Convention
& Exhibition Centre originally opened its doors to the
world in 1988, when it became Asia's largest such facility.
Then, the government granted the site to the Hong Kong
Trade Development Council which negotiated a build/
operate/transfer deal with New World Consortium, who
built two hotels - the Grand Hyatt and the New World
Harbour View - in the two towers on top. Singapore,
Hong Kong's perennial competitor, soon countered with its
own newer, larger centre. This time, the government paid
for the entire project which will be run by the HKTDC as
one unit and will once again surpass Singapore. Behind it is
the 78-storey Central Plaza, one of Asia's tallest buildings.

Above
Hong Kong Convention & Exhibition Centre
Atop a massive skeleton of steel trusses, a spectacular
sweeping roof will soar above a 100-foot glass curtain wall.
Likened to either an eagle or a plane, the roof is designed
to convey the idea of something in flight, symbolizing Hong
Kong taking off as a major financial centre of the world. At
the top level, the roof has a span of 81 metres, without
column support. While most of the materials were made
in the UK, the roof trusses were assembled in the
Philippines and shipped to Hong Kong. Here they are seen
being unloaded from barges in the harbour. The New
World Harbour View Hotel is on the right.

Left
Happy Valley and Causeway Bay Between Wanchai, dominated by the circular Hopewell Centre, and Causeway Bay is Happy Valley, home to Hong Kong's oldest horseracing venue. The first races were held in Happy Valley in 1846 on land reclaimed from a malaria-ridden swamp. Today the stands are packed every Wednesday during the season from September to May–horseracing is the territory's only legal form of gambling and thus Hong Kong's most popular spectator sport. Saturday meetings are also held, at the Hong Kong Jockey Club's other sophisticated racecourse in Shatin, in the New Territories. A percentage of the billions of dollars wagered is given to charity, making the Hong Kong Jockey Club one of the territory's most generous benefactors.

Right
Happy Valley Apart from its famous racecourse (left), Happy Valley is now a pleasant residential district, with a surprising number of green areas and sports facilities. In the foreground is the Hong Kong Jockey Club's green-roofed main clubhouse. The twin arcs of the new Hong Kong Stadium, scene of the annual Hong Kong Rugby Sevens, can be seen in the centre, behind winding Broadwood Road and in front of So Kong Po sports ground. Beyond that, bordering the Causeway Bay Typhoon Shelter, is Victoria Park, a popular place for locals to practise their *tai chi* exercises. The lower slopes of Braemar Hill border Happy Valley's east side at upper right, with Kai Tak's runway jutting into the harbour beyond.

Left
Causeway Bay The controversial Hong Kong Stadium, with its two sound-enhancing shells, dominates the end of the So Kong Po Recreation Ground at left, and the smaller South China Athletic Association Stadium to its right. This view looks straight up Wong Nai Chung Gap, thus featuring all the residences most affected by the stadium's high noise levels. Despite frequent debates over its public services, Hong Kong remains basically well-managed. The government-run Tung Wah Eastern Hospital, with its four wings at the end of the recreation ground, typifies a remarkably inexpensive public health service that overall provides good quality basic care.

Right
Towards Repulse Bay Behind Jardine's Lookout, Hong Kong Parkview sits amidst the Tai Tam Country Park, with its many hillside paths. Wong Nai Chung Gap, with the Hong Kong Cricket Club clearly visible, connects the upper reaches of Happy Valley at lower right with Repulse Bay and Stanley Headland, at upper left. The estates of Shouson Hill can be seen beyond the clouds at right.

Left
Wong Nai Chung Gap Looking from around green-clad Mount Nicholson at left are residences which can claim to be out of sight of, yet within a short drive of, the urban business district. The camera here looks from above Wong Nai Chung Gap towards the north. The Hong Kong Tennis Centre and, just in front of it, the greens of the Hong Kong Cricket Club, claim prime position along the road towards Repulse Bay and the southern side of the island. If one wishes to forsake the roads, Jardine's Lookout, extending to the right, provides a number of excellent walking trails. Central Plaza, meanwhile, pierces the skyline on the other side of Mount Nicholson.

Left
Causeway Bay This view of Causeway Bay dramatises much of what makes Hong Kong what it is today. Here highways tangle and untangle themselves to connect the south, east and west side of the island with Kowloon and the New Territories via the always busy Cross-Harbour Tunnel. The Cargo Loading Basin with its colourful lighters supplies a crucial link in the trading process, still the lifeblood of the territory. For recreation, nothing surpasses an excursion to remote bays in your own boat, an avocation which the Royal Hong Kong Yacht Club, at the end of Kellet Island, especially caters to. Meanwhile, the Police Officer's Club, to the left of the tunnel entrance, serves some of those who serve the public.

Right
Victoria Park Causeway Bay, once a natural feature of the island's intricate shoreline, has long since become the epitome of managed traffic, safe boat anchorages, and recreational grounds for the urban population. Victoria Park has its own magic, though, especially for those who wander its paths in the evenings, when park benches become small oases of privacy for lovers, and tennis and football enthusiasts play under the lights. For any that might wonder, the grey square building by the entrance to the Island Eastern Corridor houses yet more infrastructure: the Causeway Bay electrical substation.

■ Left
Causeway Bay In Hong Kong's most famous shopping mecca, Causeway Bay, pride of place must now be claimed by Times Square at centre. Boasting its own new entrance to the underground Mass Transit Railway station, it certainly demonstrates that Causeway Bay will long remain a tourist attraction. If one has any doubts, note the two-winged structure at the corner of Victoria Park: the recently opened Regal Hong Kong Hotel. The refreshing leafy green of Leighton Hill gently rises just below the Hongkong Telecom logo, while the roadway towards the Aberdeen Tunnel curves around to the bottom left. Tsim Sha Tsui East is visible directly across the harbour.

■ Above
Causeway Bay The face of Causeway Bay always changes. Just opposite the entrance to the Cross-harbour Tunnel are two new silvery towers. The Top Glory Tower is at left, with Sino Plaza, brought to you by the same company as Central Plaza, to its immediate right. As for the plethora of advertising logos, the familiar brand names of Fuji, Sharp, Citizen, and Nikon have now been joined by that of the already ubiquitous 'Cup Noodles', a more humble product of the Japanese powerhouse.

Left
North Point towards Quarry Bay North Point once made the record books as the most crowded district on the planet. Today, the Island Eastern Corridor sweeps around the promontory altogether, just as the increasing demand for prime new office space in Quarry Bay seems, at least momentarily, to have passed North Point by. The mirrored K. Wah Centre and the Kodak House in the middle distance, for instance, are more in Quarry Bay than North Point. Aloof on the slopes above, Braemar Hill Mansions overlook the city; Braemar Hill was once more grandly if inappropriately named Mount Bremer, to honour a British commodore.

Right
Quarry Bay Looking towards North Point from above Tai Koo Shing demonstrates how attractive urban development can be, as evidenced by Quarry Bay Park laced with intricate highway patterns and bright colours. Quarry Bay has now become more than just another nice place to live. Increasingly major companies are moving their offices here, filling such new complexes as Taikoo Place, the tall black and white buildings at centre. Nearby the vehicular entrance to the Eastern Harbour Crossing provides quick access to Lam Tin, Kwun Tong, and the airport at Kai Tak.

■ Left

Tai Koo Shing One enters Tai Koo Shing from the Island Eastern Corridor by passing between the twin portals of City Plaza Three and Four, the latest additions to the large shopping centre and office complex. For those who live in this mini-city of highrise dwellers, Mount Parker and Mount Butler to the right provide an opportunity to escape the urban environment. Mount Parker Road actually winds its way to the saddle between the two peaks before descending to Tai Tam on the other side of the island, while passing through country park land and skirting several reservoirs. Older Chinese have long taken advantage of the early morning hours to walk up the road to greet their friends and perform their daily exercises.

■ Right

Quarry Bay The Island Eastern Corridor curves around the end of Tai Koo Shing heading towards less-modernised districts such as Shau Kei Wan and Chai Wan. Quarries already existing when the British arrived gave Quarry Bay its name; by the late 19th century it was the site of a large sugar works. The Taikoo Dockyards arrived in the first decade of the new century, and remained an important ship maintenance centre for seventy years, before the economic advantages of multi level landuse made the construction of Tai Koo Shing all but inevitable.

Left
Shek O On the island's eastern end, Shek O
accommodates contrasting lifestyles. Plush residences on
the headland, guaranteeing privacy for those who wish it,
contrast sharply with the lively original village, with its
population of Chinese commuters and villagers, Thais, and
some westerners. Good restaurants, a beautifully
maintained tiny Tin Hau temple, Chinese-style houses and
small alleys make Shek O worth discovering, as does the
beach. Beyond the village, the Shek O Country Club
caters to the affluent with its golfing greens overlooking
the sea.

Above
Tai Tam The Hong Kong International School, one of
the network of American Schools established world-wide,
prides itself on its innovative methods. It provides
education from elementary to high school level, and
though expensive has a waiting list of children from all
nationalities. To the left of the school, the Boy Scouts
maintain a campsite and sea activities centre. The village
of Lan Nai Wan Tsuen sits along Tai Tam harbour, with only
steps to connect it to Shek O road far above. Between the
village and the road, a section of the Hong Kong Trail runs
alongside the catchwater.

Right
Tai Tam Country Park Hong Kong's reservoirs define the colour aquamarine. The Tai Tam Reservoir, in the country park of the same name, overlooks the end of Tai Tam Harbour. Tai Tam Road crosses the dam; the reservoir was once just a further extension of the harbour, with the small village of Tai Tam Tuk, long since underwater, at its head. At bottom the Hong Kong trail follows the eastern side of the inlet. The trail, divided into eight sections, meanders its way across the island, beginning at The Peak, looping around towards Aberdeen and eventually reaching its end at Big Wave Bay on the east coast.

Below right
Tai Tam A narrow strip of land along this steep and rocky coastline to the west of Tai Tam Bay accommodates single-family dwellings, apartment blocks, and one of Hong Kong's premier and most unusual country clubs, with enough room left over for Tai Tam Road. The Country Club facility of The American Club has no golf course, but it does offer members a unique alternative venue for relaxation that complements the Town Club in Exchange Square. Ever since motor roads first ringed the island in the 1920's, those seeking splendid isolation have built houses along this coast, which has often been compared to the Mediterranean.

Left
Redhill, towards Stanley Under a moody sky, Tai Tam Road winds past yet more opportunities to live overlooking the beautiful South China Sea, heading towards Stanley Peninsula in the distance. Located just to the west of Tai Tam Bay, this headland doubtlessly once had its own name, but now it is simply the 'Redhill Peninsula', after the Redhill project which encompasses it. Stanley village, with the beach, sits astride the neck of its peninsula; the headland beyond is the southern-most tip of Hong Kong Island.

Left
Chung Hom Kok These residences continue the expansion of a very old human settlement, the village of Stanley. In 1841 Stanley, famous for being the beneficiary of pirate Cheung Po Tsai's gift of a bell and drum to the local Tin Hau temple, was the island's largest village with 2,000 residents. Today, Lung Yan Court and Ma Hang Estate's brown towers, at left, are the newest additions to this landscape: they overlook the original village at the northern end of Stanley Bay. A quite different type of community sits not far away, behind the new estates, in the Ma Hang Prison. Stanley Prison is the large rectangular compound to the right of the modern-day town.

Right
South Bay After a hard day's work, one can do far worse than relax in a flat overlooking the sea as the sun sets in the west. With a beach close by, one might wonder why anyone would need a swimming pool, but a crowded summer's weekend makes a private pool quite appealing. To the left is Middle Bay, and behind can be seen the two mountains known appropriately enough as The Twins. The road behind these residences links South Bay to Stanley, only two kilometres away

Left
Repulse Bay The Bay used to be famous for the luxury hotel of the same name. Today, the hotel is gone, replaced by a replica of its original restaurant. Io the back, The Repulse Bay, owned by the original owners of the hotel, sits with a hole in the middle. The Sky Garden in the aperture offers residents and their guests an unusual place to sit outside and enjoy the stunning views. It was not until after Repulse Bay was connected to the north of the island by motor road in 1917 that it became a favoured residential area, with the wealthy building villas overlooking its shore. The first high-rise tower arrived in 1963, and before long the villas had all been torn down to make way for today's skyline of luxury apartment buildings.

Right
Repulse Bay Hong Kong's most popular beach at Repulse Bay receives constant improvements, such as this breakwater recently added to extend the enclosed safety area, and new lifeguard lookout posts. The colourful pagoda provides a quaint reminder that the territory is, after all, Chinese at heart. Once the preferred enclave to escape to for the well-to-do elite, the summer crowds which now flock to the beach here offer evidence of the constantly improving quality of life for the majority of Hong Kong's people.

Left
Deepwater Bay The Deepwater Bay Golf Course has not disappeared. This shot dramatises how dry grass can become by late winter: the 'greens' have simply changed colour. The Seaview Promenade makes for a pleasant walk along the bay. Above the beach are the homes of Shouson Hill, named for Sir Shouson Chow, the first Chinese appointed to the Executive Council in 1926. Other residences line the Repulse Bay Road which winds up toward Wong Nai Chung Gap between Mount Nicholson at left and Jardine's Lookout.

Right
Ocean Park Hong Kong's largest recreational park features some rather intriguing artforms. The roller coaster resembles the sinuous form of the rather fierce sea dragon for which it is named, while the rocky pool at left, the Wave Cove, reminds one of an aquatic Japanese rock garden. Ocean Park is yet another example of how the Royal Hong Kong Jockey Club has changed the Hong Kong landscape, others being Victoria Park, Kowloon Park, Hong Kong Park, the University of Science and Technology and the Jubilee Sports Centre. The club launched Ocean Park on the previously unoccupied peninsula in 1977; it later became a private corporation.

▌Left and Above
Aberdeen Typhoon Shelter Since water plays such an important role in Hong Kong's geography, anchorages for boats are much in demand. This is the Aberdeen South Typhoon Shelter, with Sham Wan in the foreground, and Po Chong Wan beyond it. The three floating restaurants, of course, are famous for their *dim sum*, though they never move from their moorings. The Aberdeen Marina Club is at left with its swimming pool. At upper right, fishing boats are being built on Ap Lei Chau island, a centre for the construction and repair of many types of small vessels, including junks, and the breaking up of ships for scrap.

▌Left
Aberdeen Aberdeen Harbour at lower right, once a haven for pirate ships, still provides moorings for fishing vessels which also serve as homes for their owners. Aberdeen itself, though highly urbanised and industrialised, remains close to the nature trails around the Aberdeen Reservoir at lower left. Note also the cemetery at bottom. Residents enjoy easy access to Shouson Hill, at centre left overlooking Deepwater Bay, and Repulse Bay and Stanley in the distance. The headland on which Ocean Park sits can be seen in the middle distance.

Left
Pok Fu Lam Looking down the west side of the island, the playing fields at lower left and the round residential towers service the University of Hong Kong. Baguio Villas sit at upper right near the site of the original dairy farm which first supplied Hong Kong with clean, disease-free milk in 1886; midway between them and the round towers is the Northcote College of Education. The Wah Fu Estates, at far right, are located over what remains of a once beautiful waterfall; an early 1839 survey map identified it simply as a 'Cascade of good water'.

Right
Mount Davis This peaceful view reminds one a bit of Hong Kong Island in its heyday as a Royal Colony: note the colonial-style building at left. Victoria Road slips around the corner of Mount Davis, seemingly a world away from the urban development of Kennedy Town on the mountain's other side. Flame trees provide a brilliant scarlet counterpoint to the verdant hillside vegetation. Behind the three apartment towers can be seen the platform for an old gun battery.

Above
Hong Kong Island Unlike the huge container vessels and tankers which frequent the modern cargo terminals around Kwai Chung, smaller vessels still handle significant amounts of shipping. This view encompasses the western end of the island. From Green Island at left, the towers of Kennedy Town are followed by the largely undeveloped Mount Davis, the low peak below the higher and sharper High West. Moving south, the Queen Mary Hospital dominates the skyline behind some of the facilities of Hong Kong University. Baguio Villas sits above the shoreline. On the southern end are the Wah Fu Estates, one of the earliest government housing projects. Lamma Island is at far right.

Right
Kennedy Town High West towers over Belcher's Bay, as the camera looks from above Kennedy Town towards Shek Tong Tsui. The bay's name honours the captain of the *HMS Sulphur* who landed at Possession Point to claim the island for Britain in 1841. The chute into the bay loads cement onto barges, while at far left the reclamation at Sai Ying Pun proceeds, thus continuing a process which began almost the moment Belcher stepped on Hong Kong soil. The hillside reinforcement at the base of Mount Davis testifies to the dangerous landslides to which this entire area is prone.

Construction of the Western Harbour Tunnel
Hong Kong engineers have a wealth of experience in constructing immersed tube tunnels. The new Western Harbour Tunnel between Western District and the West Kowloon Reclamation comprises 12 massive, 35,000-tonne sections containing six lanes for road traffic. The reinforced concrete sections were cast in a former quarry at Shek-O, in southeast Hong Kong Island. They were then towed to Junk Bay, in eastern Kowloon, for final checks before being tugged across the harbour and lowered into place.

Right
Western District Once one of the oldest and most traditional areas of Hong Kong, Western has been transformed by high-rise development over the past decade as rents skyrocket in Central District beyond. In front of the distinctive red and black Shun Tak Centre is the Macau Ferry Terminal, from which high-speed ferries ply the 65 kilometres across the Pearl River estuary to the Portuguese enclave. At bottom left is the entrance to the new, two kilometre Western Harbour Tunnel which will provide access to the west and south of Hong Kong Island, easing congestion at the two existing harbour crossings. The tunnel is one of a number of key projects associated with the development of Hong Kong's new airport at Chek Lap Kok.

Above
Victoria Peak Here it is, the famous Peak in close-up. To the right of the square pavilion is the Victoria Peak Garden, while below is the Governor's Walk, one of several trails around the actual summit. In 1810, this mountain was named Tai Ping Shan meaning Pacific Peak, upon the surrender of the pirate Cheung Po Tsai. At only 552 metres, the Peak is not really much more than a large hill, but for Hong Kong people it will always be special.

KOWLOON

■ Above
Tsim Sha Tsui This traditional view of Tsim Sha Tsui shows all the recognisable landmarks, from the clock tower in front of the Cultural Centre, the piers of the famed Star Ferry, the Regent Hotel with its promenade jutting out into the harbour at right, the colourful lighters which unload ships next to the empty landfill, and Kwun Tong district in the distance. Even the same old quarry defaces one of the mountains to the east of Kowloon. Still, the Clock Tower, which first told the time back in 1921, already stands witness to many amazing changes which are radically transforming Kowloon yet again.

■ Right
Tsim Sha Tsui Looking southwest over Tsim Sha Tsui, Kowloon Park provides a pleasant oasis of landscaped trees and shrubs. A recreational centre and an indoor Olympic-size swimming pool occupy its northern end; Hong Kong's only mosque is at the southeast corner. On the far side of the peninsula, the twin towers of the Gateway appear to dominate China Hong Kong City to their right. In the waters beyond, vessels navigate in an increasingly narrow channel as reclamation encroaches into Victoria Harbour. In the background, Victoria Peak, often shrouded in cloud, looms over the dramatic north shore of Hong Kong Island.

The Harbour The Discovery Bay hovercraft races tired residents home after a day at work: its twenty-minute quick commute is one reason why Disco Bay residents enjoy living there. If it appears to be headed in the wrong direction, that is because the craft must swing around the new piers jutting out into the harbour for the other outlying islands. Highlighted in the background are from left Ocean Terminal with a cruise liner docked, the Star Ferry Pier and the Cultural Centre.

Tsim Sha Tsui The setting sun highlights one of the most visible changes to Kowloon: the new tall towers which suddenly are sprouting everywhere above the once flat skyline. The Peninsula's new tower catches the sun's last rays at right, while The Gateway soars over the square Omni Prince Hotel to its right and, three buildings further on, the Omni Marco Polo Hotel. The distinctive round faces of Sutton, Craigie and Barnton Courts which once occupied the waterfront in front of the hotels have now disappeared. Ocean Terminal appears much the same, but even it no longer is cluttered with shipping containers on its near end.

Left

Kowloon The new Kowloon is dramatically visible here. With the Western Land Reclamation and Stonecutters Island (now connected to the mainland via Terminal Eight) as backdrop, Hong Kong's grandest old hotel, The Peninsula, has been totally transformed by a new tower ascending far above the once maximum building height of only 200 feet. For safety reasons, only twin-engined helicopters can land on its two helipads. To the left are the rarely glimpsed green environs of the Kowloon Police Headquarters. At bottom, ground openings provide the only evidence of what will be an underground parking and shopping complex beneath a new Salisbury Garden.

Right

Nathan Road This view offers a different perspective looking south along the Golden Mile, as Nathan Road is known. Kowloon Park is at centre, with the tall white Hong Kong Boy Scouts Centre just in front of it. Gascoigne Road curves toward the left, past the Eaton Hotel at the corner with Nathan Road, while the emerald green of the Kowloon Cricket Club appears to the left. The buildings of old Mongkok can be seen angling off at right, its street names redolent with history. Shanghai Street, Temple Street and Battery Street are where one finds the famed Jade Market and the Temple Street night market. The hotels and shopping centres of Tsim Sha Tsui East border the shore at upper left.

Left
Star Ferry Terminal The famous green and white ferries of the Star Ferry Company have provided an invaluable transport link across the harbour between Hong Kong Island and Kowloon since 1898. Today the eight-minute ride is also a top attraction for tourists. At HK$2, first class, for a panoramic view of Victoria Harbour, this must be the cheapest sightseeing ride in the world! Luxury cruise liners moor at Ocean Terminal: this photograph shows the Canberra on its annual visit to Hong Kong. Looking somewhat incongruous at the tip of the Kowloon peninsula is the clock tower, all that remains of the original Kowloon-Canton railway terminus. Beside it is the futuristic Hong Kong Cultural Centre.

Right
Nathan Road Now this is a truly picturesque view of the Golden Mile at its best, with the designed 'natural' artforms of Kowloon Park nicely set off by the white elegance of the Kowloon Mosque on its corner. Notice the twisting walkway atop the Park Lane Shopper's Boulevard, a row of elegant shops on the west side of Nathan Road. Nathan Road is named for Governor Sir Matthew Nathan, who built the road at the turn of the century; critics dubbed it Nathan's Folly, because of the unpromising outlook for the peninsula's future.

Right
Tsim Sha Tsui The controversial Hong Kong Cultural Centre, nicknamed the "ski jump", was opened in 1989. Built on the site of the old Kowloon-Canton Railway station, it boasts a 2,100-seat Concert Hall, a 1,750-seat Grand Theatre, and a smaller Studio Theatre. Next to it on the waterfront, in matching salmon tiles, is the Hong Kong Museum of Art. Opposite the domed Space Museum, which houses one of the world's largest and technically most sophisticated planetariums, stand three hotels: the Salisbury YMCA, the Peninsula with its new tower and helipad, and the Sheraton. The North Point area of Hong Kong Island is in shadow.

Left
Tsim Sha Tsui Brown and green: these are the complementary colours of the hotel, shopping and office complex at the tip of Tsim Sha Tsui, and the vegetation of Signal Hill Garden. Signal Tower, in the garden, once dropped a large, hollow copper ball to signal the time so that ships could set their chronometers. A promenade curves around the New World Centre and Regent Hotel complex from Tsim Sha Tsui East to the Star Ferry. Ocean Terminal juts toward the top of the picture, next to the horseshoe-shaped Ocean Centre, while cloud-enshrouded Victoria Peak appears on Hong Kong Island.

Below
New World Centre Looking straight down, one sees both the gloriously situated swimming pools and lounging areas, and the rather more pragmatic vents and other devices which appear on most roofs. The Regent Hotel is at left, and the New World Centre and Hotel, with its own swimming pool, at upper right. This photograph was taken in the late afternoon: the photographer stood on the helicopter's strut, bravely holding the camera pointed down in front of him, without quite daring to look through the lens.

Kowloon Most of Kowloon spreads before the eye, from the original harbour between it and Hong Kong Island, north to Ho Man Tin at right. Gascoigne Road crosses the peninsula behind the brown buildings housing the Polytechnic University. To its right lies the King's Park Sports Ground: the hill at the edge of the photograph is King's Park Rise. The low buildings to the right of Gascoigne Road include the former Gun Club Hill Barracks. The freight terminal at bottom demonstrates the continuing need for lighters, as the small barges with cranes are called, to off load containers: they are transferred here to freight trains heading for China.

Above

Hung Hom The traffic entering the north entrance of the original Cross Harbour Tunnel passes by the hotels of Tsim Sha Tsui East to the left and the Hong Kong Coliseum, manifesting the 'form-follows-function' school of design, to the right. Behind the Coliseum, the Hung Hom terminus of the Kowloon-Canton Railway services both passenger and freight traffic. At lower left, the Grand Stanford Harbour View overlooks the pedestrian overpass, with the Nikko Hotel nestled in the road's curve next to it. Kai Tak's tarmac is at upper right.

Right

Hung Hom While some hotels in Hong Kong, such as the Hilton and the Hotel Victoria, close down, new ones open up, often in more outlying districts. The four star Harbour Plaza Hotel opened in 1995 at the tip of Hung Hom. Behind it stretch various residential developments including Whampoa Gardens and Whampoa Estates. To the right, the public Tai Wan Shan Swimming Pools, and the accompanying recreation grounds, provide much welcome opportunities for physical exercise and sports.

▌Left
Kowloon City With the Hong Kong International
Airport in the distance, Nga Tsin Wai Road bends behind a
swimming pool before reaching the airport, while at upper
right Argyle Street heads in the same direction from the
southwest. In between, Boundary Street, to the left,
converges with Prince Edward Road. The half-circle at
bottom which breaks up the pattern is Essex Crescent. At
the moment, all major roads in Kowloon City lead to Kai
Tak, but in 1998 the airport will close, raising the intriguing
question of what changes will happen to this historic
district in the future.

▌Above
Kowloon Tong Looking in the opposite direction,
from right above Kowloon Tsai Park at bottom, the eye
follows the flight path of planes taking off from Kai Tak to
the west, over Stonecutters Island, green, Terminal Eight
next to it, and the northern end of the West Kowloon
Reclamation. Wonderland Villas crest the hill at upper right.
To the left of the shrub-covered hill is the oval of Mongkok
Stadium: the Kowloon-Canton Railway line curves in front
of it across the entire photograph. Kowloon Tong station,
where the KCR and the Mass Transit Railway intersect,
occupies the large building to the right.

Left
Kai Tak The tarmac here appears rather calm, belying the reality that Kai Tak's international airport is one of the world's busiest, and already operating well over its designed capacity several years before the scheduled opening of the new Chek Lap Kok airport. Prince Edward Road points straight away from the terminal towards the top of the picture. Splashes of fluorescent colour, such as on the buildings at right, contrast strongly with the bland tones and monotonous repetition characterising so much of the urban landscape.

Above
Diamond Hill Setting a magnificent backdrop for Kai Tak, this range of mountains separates the Kowloon peninsula from the rest of the mainland almost as definitively as the harbour separates the island from Kowloon. These peaks are eight of the 'nine dragons' for which Kowloon was named; the last one was the fugitive Song emperor. Lion Rock sits proudly at left, while vehicular traffic heads towards the Tate's Cairn Tunnel, over two kilometres of highway cutting through the heart of the mountains on its way to Sha Tin. Back on the airport tarmac, the air cargo terminal is at bottom.

Right
Kwun Tong Adjacent to the Kwun Tong Mass Transit Railway station, Yuet Wah Street swings sharply through an older section of urban Hong Kong. Despite the dramatic images of gleaming new office towers and picturesquely-situated luxury developments, the typical Hong Kong resident is more likely to work in nondescript office buildings such as these, commuting by bus or MTR train, and enjoying the amenities of the local park or rooftop basketball court.

Left
Kowloon Bay More colours, this time of aircraft livery on the apron which runs adjacent to the runway and of new buildings with imaginative owners, enliven this view looking eastward towards the quarry at top. The bright blue building is a waste disposal plant. The elevated Kwun Tong Bypass runs east along the edge of Kowloon Bay before turning inland at Lam Tin.

Above
Yau Tong Beyond the Eastern Harbour Crossing and the airport at Kai Tak, the urban expanse which is Kowloon reaches its eastern periphery beneath Devil's Peak, as a Cathay Pacific airliner in its old livery takes off for distant destinations. Hidden behind Devil's Peak is Rennie's Mill and the Junk Bay New Town. The village at right is Sam Ka Tsuen, with its own typhoon shelter. Just to the east of this view is the Lei Yue Mun gap, the harbour's narrowest passage.

NEW TERRITORIES

Tsing Yi and Tsuen Wan The three faces of Tsing Yi Island dramatically show themselves at centre: the original green-clad island, the relatively long-standing residential district on the east, and the industrial side to the west and south. Now, the construction of the new bridge will likely transform Tsing Yi even further. To the left is Tsuen Wan beneath Beacon Hill, surrounding the striking reddish tower, with container ports now extending all the way to Stonecutters Island. Beyond, the dramatic peak skyline of Hong Kong Island lies revealed, much as the first Western visitors must have seen it. From right, the lowly Mount Davis, High West, and Victoria Peak with all its buildings overlook Western and Central districts. Mount Butler and Mount Parker are on the left end, beyond the brown scar of the quarry. Lamma Island appears at right.

Left

Kwai Chung Hong Kong's container port at Kwai Chung, in eastern Kowloon, is the busiest in the world, handling some 12.6 million 20-foot equivalent units (TEUs) in 1995. This vast and highly efficient port is vital not just for Hong Kong but also for southern China, one of the world's fastest industrializing areas. Some 65% of cargo passing through Hong Kong is entrepôt trade with China. Eight terminals now extend as far as Stonecutters Island, cutting off the four-metre channel which once separated it from the mainland. A new naval base for the Chinese garrison is being built on the island. Snaking through the Kowloon peninsula is the new West Kowloon Expressway, designed to provide a fast road link to the new airport at Chek Lap Kok.

Right

Kwai Chung Looking down at Terminal Five reminds one of a giant toy erector set with brightly-painted containers as huge Lego blocks. Like Japanese tatami mats, each container is exactly the same size and shape, thus enabling the automation of loading, unloading and storing; the average ship turn-around time is an amazing twelve hours, compared with two-and-a-half days by traditional methods. In the distance is Terminal Six, situated between the Hongkong International Terminals building and Terminal Eight painted in a predominant red.

Left
Stonecutters Island The western end of Terminal Eight, the newest to be constructed, sits attached to Stonecutters Island. The island has since the last century been an off-limits military depot which also featured a rich variety of animal life, such as nesting kites, pythons, and fish-eating cormorants. In 1994 it even hosted an extremely rare visitor to Hong Kong, the hoopoe, a strange crested bird whose flight resembles that of a butterfly. Unfortunately, these containers, many marked Hyundai from Korea, indicate the wave of the future for Stonecutters and all of its denizens.

Left
Ma Wan Ma Wan Island once sat just off the northeast corner of Lantau in quiet isolation. Even today, it remains one of the designated floating fish farm sites, usually located in more remote bays around the territory. Note that the village at left, Tin Liu, rather resembles a modern suburban development, especially when compared with the more traditionally chaotic village at right. Tsing Yi and the new bridge construction dominate behind Ma Wan, and Terminal Eight can be seen just around the edge of Tsing Yi's green hills. Hong Kong Island appears at upper right.

Right
Tai Lam Country Park Busy Tuen Mun Road
connects urban Tsuen Wan to urban Tuen Mun, just two
kilometres to the west of this view. Castle Peak Road runs
just below it for local drivers. Beyond, though, Tai Lam
Chung Reservoir nestles among the hills of the Tai Lam
Country Park. The famed 100 kilometre MacLehose Trail
winds along the north side of the reservoir. Each year
teams of four race to complete the entire trail, which runs
from near High Island Reservoir to Tuen Mun by a highly
convoluted route; the military-trained Gurkhas of Nepal
are the perennial favourites.

Left
Tuen Mun Road The new resort hotel in the New Territories, at the Gold Coast, perches at lower left, in front of the quay curving out into the sea. Pearl Island sits at the right edge. On this beautiful day, the marina is partly empty. Behind, though, sits evidence of a controversial issue which mars the landscape: shipping containers stored until needed, as they are in many locations around the New Territories. The partly barren mountains of the Tai Lam Country Park sit to the right of the reservoir at upper left, and Hong Kong Island occupies the far horizon.

Right
Castle Peak Bay Looking from high above Lung Mun Road, a large number of people occupy flats in such quaintly or wishfully-named residential developments as Butterfly Estates, Melody Garden and Miami Beach Towers. More land is being reclaimed from Castle Peak Bay, reducing the size of the typhoon shelter even further. Pearl Island juts out into the harbour, with Lantau and behind it Hong Kong at upper right. Tai Mo Shan, the territory's highest point, rises 957 metres at the upper left.

▮ Above
Tuen Mun From above Butterfly Estates, the early New Town of Tuen Mun spreads to either side of what has now become an enormous if anonymous canal, the remnants of the river which once flowed placidly into Castle Peak Bay. Tuen Mun was the first Hong Kong place to be recorded in history: it already had a garrison guarding its excellent and frequently used harbour during the Tang dynasty. Yuen Long, another of the first New Towns, sits at upper left. Shekou, the western end of the Special Economic Zone of Shenzhen in China, lies beyond the flats of Deep Bay.

▮ Right
Western New Territories From above the emerging New Town of Tin Shui Wai, this view looks southwest-ward along the very busy corridor between Yuen Long and Tuen Mun, just to the left of Castle Peak. Always an important agricultural area, this alluvial plain now is scattered with container storage yards and yet more new developments, but its vegetable farms and fish ponds remain important. In the far distance can be seen the barren level area which will soon be home to Hong Kong's new airport. The entire profile of Lantau Island appears on the horizon

▎Above
West Coast, New Territories Along the coast of
the northwestern New Territories, between the villages of
Ngau Hom Sha and Sheung Pak Nai, the reflected waters of
shrimp and fish ponds and the deep greens of summer
vegetable gardens edge along the waterfront at high tide.
The dirt road runs up towards the gunnery range north of
Castle Peak. Development encroaches even here, as
evidenced in the new construction at the base of the
mountain.

▎Right
Lau Fau Shan Shan means mountain, but to all
appearances Lau Fau Shan sits on rather flat, marshy land:
the only 'mountains' here are those of oyster shells
extending ever further into Deep Bay. Immediately west of
Tin Shui Wai and south of China across the bay, Lau Fau
Shan largely depends upon oysters and other sea food: the
oysters are either dried or made into oyster sauce. Trees
green all year around and the brown grass of winter typify
Hong Kong's semi-tropical location.

▌Above
Yuen Long The old town of Yuen Long became a
New Town in the 1970's, completely transforming this
region of traditional clan villages, such as those of the Shap
Pat Heung area in the foreground. The Tangs, the largest
New Territory clan, first occupied this district in the 11th
century, and built Hong Kong's first college. Looking
southeast, Hong Kong Island appears on the horizon at left
with Lantau to its right; a single tower of the new airport
bridge rises above the far hills.

▌Right
Nam Sang Wai The fish ponds of Nam Sang Wai
stretch toward Fairview Park at the top of the photograph.
The Pok Wai development is at upper right. Pond fish
farming has been practised in China for centuries; carp are
a favourite, with several different species in the same
pond. The little stream extending in both directions around
Fairview Park is the Kam Tin Ho, which flows west toward
Deep Bay. Note the gaggles of ducks and the viaduct
crossing the stream at bottom.

| Left
New Territories, Looking Southeast The changes in this view from that of the previous image, taken a couple of years earlier, clearly indicate the eventual fate of the fish ponds. Lam Tsuen Peak rises beyond Fairview Park. Tolo Harbour is in the distance, while Tai Mo Shan dominates the centre of the dark horizon and Yuen Long Industrial Estate sits below the river at lower right. In front of Tai Mo Shan lies the airstrip at Sek Kong, home of the 28th Squadron of the Royal Air Force, and sometime refugee camp. Kowloon and Hong Kong are at upper right.

| Above
Palm Springs This new development just above Fairview Park at bottom, demonstrates the human tendency to continually dominate and transform the environment. Note the rather incongruous swimming pool in the midst of the surrounding waters of the fish ponds. Just to the upper left of the pool is the tiny village of Wo Shang Wai, engulfed entirely by the new development; for some reason the villagers decided not to sell out. A fish pond originally surrounded the village on all sides, making it a virtual island, which of course it still is. Castle Peak Highway heads toward Fanling at top.

Left
Mai Po Marshes The Mai Po Marshes are shown on many maps as a large stretch of ponds in the northwest corner of the territory. Actually, most of the water fills commercial fish ponds, and the Mai Po Marshes Nature Reserve occupies the relatively small but clearly defined swath of water and land to the left of Fairview Park. It also includes the green carpet of mangrove thickets extending out toward the mudflats of Deep Bay, and hosts thousands of migratory birds every year; over 250 species have been sighted here. In the distance lies Shenzhen, including its as yet completely undeveloped western district beyond the nature reserve.

Above
Shenzhen Like a new and growing young sister to Hong Kong, Shenzhen rises above the fish ponds of the New Territories. Note the many new tall buildings, especially at centre. The Shenzhen Special Economic Zone, like Hong Kong a territory more than a single city, has three million people of its own, and maintains its own water supply through reservoirs similar to those in Hong Kong. China sells Hong Kong over half of its freshwater supply each year from reserves such as the Shenzhen Reservoir seen here.

■ Left
Fanling Close to China, the intriguing layout of one
of the three golf courses at Fanling reminds one of a maze.
At centre the New Town of Sheung Shui is the last stop on
the Kowloon-Canton Railway before the border station at
Lo Wu. Shenzhen, China, spreads out at upper left, while
to the right is Fanling New Town, also on the railway. At
top centre, Robin's Nest with its summit cloaked in clouds,
rises 492 metres less than two kilometres from China, with
only Starling Inlet and Mirs Bay beyond at upper right.

■ Above
New Territories, Looking Northeast The Tai Po
Road and the railway cross the countryside towards
Fanling at left. The residential estate of Hong Lok Yuen sits
just in front of a small mountain named, appropriately,
Cloudy Hill. To the right the mountains of Pat Sing Leng
Country Park extend eastward, in front of Starling Inlet
and Mirs Bay. The controversial nuclear power plant of
Daya Bay, in China, can be seen in the upper right corner.
A new development of China's Shenzhen Special
Economic Zone extends to the left of Robin's Nest, which
sits in shadow ten kilometres in the distance.

Left
Lok Ma Chau More than one road leads to China these days. Supplementing the road and rail crossing into Shenzhen from Lo Wu at top, the busy Lok Ma Chau border crossing is accessed by the highway that turns off the Castle Peak Road, at far left. But it was not always so easy to cross this border; during the heyday of the Cultural Revolution, visitors to Hong Kong ascended to the lookout point on Lok Ma Chau hill, just beyond the road, for a glimpse of mysterious 'Red China'. At right, the Royal Hong Kong Jockey Club operates the Beas River Country Club. Kai Kung Leng peak dominates the country park of the same name at bottom.

Right
Beas River Looking towards the southwest, the Beas River Country Club caters to just about everyone associated with The Royal Hong Kong Jockey Club, including the horses, who are housed in the octagonal stable complex. Beas River incorporates training facilities, but also offers members an opportunity to escape the urban environment and enjoy club amenities. Adjacent to the club is one of the 18-hole golf courses near Fanling run by the Royal Hong Kong Golf Club.

Left
Tai Po Tolo Harbour, famed for its pearl fisheries in the centuries before British rule, today suffers from the bane of all major cities: pollution. The continual expansion of the Tai Po Industrial Estate, beyond the New Town of Tai Po, contributes to the problem, as surely does the unofficial 'new town' at the foot of Ma On Shan at right. Likewise, suburban developments like Hong Lok Yuen, at left, require a greater dependence on automobiles than the average Hong Kong residence.

Right
Towards Tai Po A traffic jam on a cloudy late Sunday afternoon slows travel considerably for those travelling south, while lanes in the opposite direction are frustratingly open. Meanwhile, those travelling on the Kowloon-Canton Railway enjoy a dependably-scheduled service between Sheung Shui and Hung Hom. Suburban developments, such as Hong Lok Yuen at upper centre, and rural villages, with houses scattered about in a pleasingly random fashion, dominate the rural landscapes of the mid-New Territories. Tai Po peeks above the hills at top.

▌ Above
Tai Po Kau From above Lead Mine Pass, the Tai Po Kau Nature Reserve covers the hillsides south of Tai Po. A true tropical forest in ecological terms, Tai Po Kau thus hosts a rich variety of tree species, flourishing side by side. As one climbs toward its higher altitudes, the number of species dramatically decreases. Beyond the forest, the Chinese University, the southern end of Tolo Harbour, and the Ma On Shan urban centre can be seen.

▌ Left
Tolo Highway The railroad to China and its accompanying highway round the headland from Sha Tin towards Tai Po, in the distance below the mountains of Pat Sin Leng Country Park. First constructed in 1912 to connect Hong Kong with Canton (now known as Guangzhou) in China, the railway was privatised and electrified in the early eighties. In addition to providing passenger and freight service to China, the Kowloon-Canton Railway also operates a local commuter service between Kowloon and the growing urban centres of the mid-New Territories.

Left
Sha Tin Along the now completely tamed Shing Mun River, once was simply a sandy cove surrounded by rural villages. Land reclamation filled in much of the bay, and the New Town has become a city of about 700,000 people rising amidst the untouched hillsides which remain close by. Along the un-named canal extending north from the Shing Mun channel is the Fo Tan district, at the foot of Cove Hill. Greenwood Terraces, with the round swimming pools at left, numbers among the many private developments which have grown up around the urban centre.

Right
Sha Tin The beginning of the Shing Mun Channel, once a naturally flowing river, lies here, adjacent to an amusement park and the old village of Tai Wai, long since engulfed by the relentless urban growth of Sha Tin New Town. During the rainy season, the culvert itself fills with water, becoming an extension of the channel. Originally Sha Tin was simply a sandy cove with numerous villages such as Tai Wai; now it is home to 700,000 people, more than Boston or Liverpool. At upper left is the Lower Shing Mun Temporary Housing Area, home to immigrants who have yet to be placed in public housing.

Below
Sha Tin This view provides a short course in Hong Kong highway markings on a typical Sha Tin intersection, but the traffic itself is revealing. The number of red urban taxis in a New Territories' city, whose taxis are green, indicates how close Sha Tin is to urban Kowloon: raising the question of whether Hong Kong is really one city, many cities close together, or something else altogether.

▌Above
Sha Tin Channel Pure geometry characterises the entrance of the Shing Mun Channel into Tolo Harbour. On the corner is the Sha Tin Sewage Treatment Works, situated in front of the Royal Hong Kong Jockey Club's stables and the Sha Tin racecourse. The road at left heads towards the Tate's Cairn Tunnel, while the Tolo Highway at right connects the Lion Rock Tunnel with Tai Po to the north.

▌Right
Ma On Shan The new unofficial 'new town' at the foot of Ma On Shan has been created by private developers on the south side of Tolo Harbour, east of Sha Tin. In addition to such luxury developments as Chevalier Garden, Villa Athena, and Sunshine City, this urban area is also home to two Temporary Housing Areas. On the peninsula beyond, the Whitehead Detention Centre houses illegal Vietnamese immigrants waiting to be repatriated to their homeland. Across the bay is the Plover Cove Reservoir.

Left
Tai Long Wan Overlooking the South China Sea towards America on Hong Kong's east side is Tai Long Wan. The little promontory is Mong Yue Kok, and the rather small collection of houses the village of Ham Tin. The fields look rather desolate, indicating that this photograph was taken in winter. Tung Wan Shan is the hill at the beginning of the peninsula at top. These beaches are accessible only by boat, or by walking across the hills of the Sai Kung East Country Park on paths like the MacLehose trail, which turns south at Ham Tin to follow the beach.

Above
Sharp Peak A close-up of the natural side of Hong Kong, Sharp Peak rises like a moss-covered dragon with its head in the clouds. To the more prosaic-minded geographer, Sharp Peak attains 468 metres in height. Many trails are available for walking here, as across all of wild Hong Kong: one walking expert suggests you could spend a lifetime of weekends hill walking and never walk the same path twice. Tai Long Wan beach is at far right.

High Island From above High Island Reservoir, the eye looks straight south across what originally was High Island, as it is incongruously still known. On the far side lies Rocky Harbour, with the floating fish rafts of Tung A village. The MacLehose Trail follows the road around the reservoir; the road ends about 3 kilometres further on at the dam which marks the east end of the man-made lake. Beyond Basalt and Bluff islands (from left) the ocean has been a firing range for the British Navy: it is likely Chinese naval vessels will use it for the same purpose, given Hong Kong's strategic location on the South China Sea.

High Island Reservoir Situated along one of Hong Kong's major sources of water, the infamous High Island Camp symbolises one of Hong Kong's current challenges: what to do about its Vietnamese refugees. The advantages of the site's isolation are obvious, as nobody resides nearby to feel threatened by escaping camp 'inmates'. Peculiarly enough, there is also a holiday camp and water sports centre at bottom left. The few windsurfers visible seem to be using the lake at centre as a sort of training pool before venturing out on the open ocean.

Left

Rocky Harbour Here is Rocky Harbour as it appears looking southwest, with Basalt and Bluff islands in the distance. These two remote villages, Tung A sticking out into the harbour, and Pak A at lower right, are perhaps home to descendants of early inhabitants of the region. They may have fled from the incoming waves of new migrants, such as the Cantonese who settled in the agricultural lowlands, or the Hakka who came later, in the 17th century.

Right

Kau Sai Chau This tiny harbour on southern Kau Sai Chau Island neatly envelops floating fish rafts and three pleasure craft moored together. The floating fish farms, while distinctive, have only come into their own in the last couple of decades. Raising both local fish captured from the open ocean and imported small fry, this bay is located in one of a number of carefully government-designated and regulated zones. The north end of Kau Sai Chau is the site of a new public golf course.

Above
Hebe Haven A boat-studded Hebe Haven, named for the *Young Hebe* survey ship, provides a secure mooring adjacent to the more open waters of Port Shelter beyond. Port Shelter's more interesting Chinese name means 'oxtail bay'. The first rows of Marina Cove houses encroach at right, while the peninsula to the left is country park, with a mixture of natural and plantation woodlands on its south side, behind the fish rafts of Ma Lam Wat. Past the peninsula at upper left sits Sharp Island, in front of Kau Sai Chau.

Right
Hebe Haven One of the great pleasures of living in Hong Kong must be the opportunity to explore the fascinating coastlines and islands on the south and east sides of the territory. Fortunately, a person need not be affluent enough to purchase one of these boats: a 'junk' or a yacht can easily be chartered for a day. One does wonder, though, at the stunning scenery which the sailors aboard the *Young Hebe* must have enjoyed in the days before New Towns and suburban planning.

Above
Nam Wai Nam Wai remained a traditional fishing village until the late seventies. Today, it is just another suburban community, though the simple, clean lines of its Chinese-style houses, rather randomly situated, provide a refreshing contrast to the sometimes offbeat designs and military-like precision of many of Hong Kong's more modern residential developments.

Right
Marina Cove The carefully-planned, sea-oriented Marina Cove faces the village of Nam Wai at low tide, across the Ho Chung stream. Marina Cove provides homes, shops, yacht berths and a clubhouse, but most importantly it sits adjacent to some of the finest sailing waters in the world. Hiram's Highway climbs toward the new Hong Kong University of Science and Technology at upper right. None of the surrounding grass and shrub-covered hillsides are protected and thus may well disappear under the developer's bulldozer within the next decade.

■ Left
Hong Kong University of Science and Technology Junk Bay New Town emerging in the upper right symbolises Hong Kong's commitment to its growing population, but the new Hong Kong University of Science and Technology represents the territory's understanding that it must become ever more technologically competitive in world markets. With schools of Science, Engineering, Business and Management, and two masters programmes, by the end of the decade the new university will enrol approximately 10,000 students.

■ Above
Silverstrand Looking above the beach at Silverstrand and the collection of privately-developed residential areas which have sprung up around it, one can see the picnic area on the little knob of land facing unpopulated Shelter Island. The verdant green peninsula beyond is part of the Clearwater Bay Country Park. With its shark net, Silverstrand Beach here rather resembles a large, if saltwater, swimming pool.

Left
Silverstrand and Junk Bay One of the third generation of such city-building projects, Junk Bay New Town was ready for its first residents as early as 1988, long before much of its extensive development had even been initiated. By the turn of the century, plans now call for this area to contain half a million people and *three* major industrial estates. In contrast, the suburban developments along Silverstrand, and the luxury home at centre overlooking Silver Terrace Road, typify a very different lifestyle.

Right
Silverstrand Beach Some were shocked in 1995 when the government refused to launch a shark-hunt after three people died in a short period in the eastern waters of the territory. Yet careful management as represented by the presumably shark-proof net serves both to protect Hong Kong people and allow the large fish the right to their ocean home.

Right
Clearwater Bay Hong Kong may not need another movie studio in the Clearwater Bay area, but this is the home of Star Television, the brainchild of the Li Ka Shing family. Hong Kong thus has become the centre of a media phenomenon which is changing the planet; Star TV brings the world to peasants in India and to newly affluent urban Chinese in nominally communist China. High Junk Peak rises at left, and its namesake New Town at upper right.

Above
Clearwater Bay The early visitor who gave the bay its name was clearly impressed, though other inlets in the eastern New Territories could equally claim the title. Unlike the brackish water of the Pearl River estuary on Hong Kong's west side, the eastern waters are true ocean, sufficiently salty to provide even poor swimmers with enough buoyancy to paddle around in. The trail in front offers a clear view of Basalt and Bluff islands, just behind the country park land on the peninsula, at upper left.

Right
Clearwater Bay Beach Hong Kong people leave their own 'native' urban or suburban environments to enjoy the sea at remote Clearwater Bay Beach. Swimming is by far the most popular form of recreation during the summer, inexpensive and relaxing. Officially, there are 42 gazetted beaches in the territory, but many people simply rent a boat, drop anchor off even more remote coasts, and dive in.

▌Above
Clearwater Bay The Clearwater Bay Country Club
with its marina chose an apt location for 18 holes of the
old Scottish game of golf, since Hong Kong's rugged coasts
have often been favourably compared to those of
Scotland. Floating fish farms add to the local colour for
golfers, as does the view of High Junk Peak, at upper
centre, in the Clearwater Bay Country Park. A beautifully
conceived and sited golf course such as this actually
enhances the surrounding environment, and provides
golfers with an opportunity to appreciate the 'other side'
of Hong Kong.

▌Right
Clearwater Bay Country Club A very sheltered
port for yachts and boats, and the Country Club's unique
angular architecture, are set against the backdrop of the
open ocean, Clearwater Bay faces straight west across the
South China Sea towards Taiwan.

Junk Peak A wish to hide away from all of urban Hong Kong and pretend it does not exist, if only for a moment... This cluster of homes seems to do just that on the slopes of Junk Peak. Even the roadway discretely winds its way behind the mountain, leaving the mountainside free for climbing and other non-urban pursuits. Very urban Chai Wan is on the other side of the harbour.

Left below
Hang Hau The government built Hang Hau at left as part of the Junk Bay New Town; somehow the architecture gives it away. In contrast, private developers created Hong Sing Garden at right. The highway sweeping from bottom left has just emerged from the Tseung Kwan O Tunnel, which connects the New Town with Kwun Tong. Junk Bay may be separated from the rest of Hong Kong by mountains, but the territory's busy construction engineers have never been fazed by challenges.

Right
Rennie's Mill How many people have heard of Rennie's Mill, the so-called last bastion of the Guomingdang (Nationalist Party) in Hong Kong, and yet not known where it is? The answer is here, across from Chai Wan, and looking like it is about to be overwhelmed by Junk Bay's new city. The Guomingdang, of course, ruled China before the Communist takeover, and still govern Taiwan. Named for W. H. Rennie who operated a mill here, the settlement's Chinese name is Tiu Keung Leng.

Next page
Lam Tin Where the highway turns in from the Kwun Tong Bypass at lower right, the Mass Transit Railway, just beneath it, passes underground into the gray building which houses the Lam Tin Station. At middle right, vehicles enter the Eastern Harbour Tunnel on its way to Quarry Bay. By contrast, the road winding around Devil's Peak in the distance actually is a dead-end, halting in a village before it reaches Rennie's Mill. The open grassy area at right mysteriously and pleasantly just seems to be there, without being a designated park or 'garden'.

OUTLYING ISLANDS

Left

Lamma Island The island appears in all its glory: sprawling, with green and brown hillsides, two villages and the Lamma Island Power Station puffing away, providing electrical energy to Hong Kong Island and Lamma. Inhabited since the stone age, Lamma today is home to a mixture of native islanders, other Hong Kong Chinese, and expatriates. The village of Yung Shue Wan sits near the power station, while So Kwu Wan is barely visible in the island's deep indentation to left, positioned beneath Lamma's highest peak. Note the shipping convoy between Lamma and the Wah Fu Estates at lower right.

Right

Yung Shue Wan Yung Shue Wan village on western Lamma Island is named for the banyan tree. The lively village is isolated by the hills beyond it from the busy harbour activity which is so close by, and the feeling of being in another world is enhanced by the ban on cars and lorries. A leisurely 35 minutes from Central by ferry, emergency transport can be provided by helicopter from the helipad at left. The Castle Peak Power Station hovers on the horizon.

Below

Lamma Island The brown hills of winter crest Lamma Island toward the south, until one reaches Mount Stenhouse, Lamma's highest peak at right. Power Station Beach, in front, and the popular Hung Shing Ye Beach, face across the western harbour. The forests at bottom surely are all planted; environmentalists sometimes sponsor community tree planting days on the island, though the barrenness of its heights holds it own beauty.

Left
Cheung Chau This island has long been the most popular outlying island for urbanites who enjoy a 'village' atmosphere; it also is base to a still large fishing community who live on their boats. The contrast between flat Cheung Chau and Lamma seems quite dramatic from this view, towards the southeast and hence away from the rest of Hong Kong. The islands on the horizon, to the south of the territory, are part of China.

Above
Cheung Chau Looking northeast, Cheung Chau's geographic position becomes dramatically clear. At upper right is the Lamma Island Power Station, and behind Lamma, of course, sits Hong Kong Island. Victoria Peak is easily recognisable because of its houses. Hei Ling Chau, home to a small population, is the island at far left, with Peng Chau beyond it, before one reaches the Kwai Chung and Tsuen Wan districts on the furthest horizon, about 12 kilometres away.

▌Above
Off Lantau Island One speedboat appears to chase another between Cheung Chau at right, Hei Ling Chau, and the tip of Lantau at left.

▌Right
Discovery Bay Like a colony on the northeast side of Lantau Island, Discovery Bay is a popular, more upmarket alternative to living on Cheung Chau or Lamma. The three vessels rounding the peninsula at right are Discovery Bay hovercraft, one of the attractions of residency, due to their high speed, frequency, and twenty-four hour service. The marina provides another benefit for boat-owners. Discovery Bay keeps expanding: the newest phase of development, La Costa, on the peninsula near the marina, quickly sold out in 1995.

| Left
Lantau Island Massive Lantau Island is over twice the size of Hong Kong Island (142 square kilometres), with 3% of the population. With its rugged terrain crowned by Lantau and Sunset Peaks, this is a hiker's paradise: more than half the island is designated as country parkland and there are than 70 kilometres of well-marked trails. The small, dumbbell-shaped island is Peng Chau, with Discovery Bay immediately to its left, on Lantau's northeast coast. Mui Wo in Silvermine Bay can be seen at right above the clouds. The new airport highway and rail corridor lies on the north side of the island, leading to the two towers of the Tsing Ma Bridge. The town in the background is Tsuen Wan, in the New Territories.

| Above
Discovery Bay Another view of Discovery Bay dramatically illustrates the advantages of living on a relatively unpopulated island, with Lantau Island's carpeted hillsides surrounding the development on two sides, and the city nowhere in sight. Residents enjoy a car-free environment, as well as a wide range of leisure facilities, including swimming pools, tennis courts, a yacht marina and an 18-hole hilltop golf course (top right, next to the reservoir), and several beautiful sandy beaches. The island of Hei Ling Chau is in the background.

| Above
Chek Lap Kok Looking much like a blank slate waiting to be written upon, the reclamation for the airport has created a new island from the levelling of Chek Lap Kok and extensive landfill. In this early view, the once isolated villages around the bay known as Tung Chung Wan remain untouched. Before long 20,000 new residents will live in the New Town to be established here on the bay, the first of many more to come. The second runway will run along the northern edge of the airport.

| Right
Chek Lap Kok Airport By mid-1996, work on the HK$10.1 billion passenger terminal of Hong Kong's new airport at Chek Lap Kok was well advanced. Featuring wide panoramic windows and a spectacular gull-wing modular roof, the structure will have a gross floor area of 500,000 square metres. The terminal's Y-shaped concourse will have 38 airbridge gates connecting aircraft to the building. In addition to more than two kilometres of moving walkways, an Automated People Mover (driverless train) will operate along the 750-metre-long central concourse. Road, rail and ferry links will ensure swift transport to the heart of Hong Kong.

Po Lin Monastery His hand raised in the traditional gesture as if offering benediction on all that Hong Kong is creating, the Temple of Heaven Buddha nevertheless reminds one that Hong Kong indeed is Asian, and always will be, whatever the developments of the twenty-first century. The world's largest seated outdoor bronze Buddha, it overlooks the important Po Lin monastery, destination of many a Hong Kong visitor and a large number of local residents on festival days. Hidden almost mysteriously behind clouds, Lantau Peak – the island's highest mountain – rises in the background.

South China Sea A solitary yacht makes its way in the waters beyond Rocky Harbour, where only a few islands dot the South China Sea. Looking southeast, Wang Chau at left, Basalt Island in the background, and Fu Tau Tan Chau surround a cluster of smaller islands. The South China Sea, of course, extends for hundreds of miles southward, until it reaches the shores of Vietnam, Malaysia and the Philippines.

INDEX

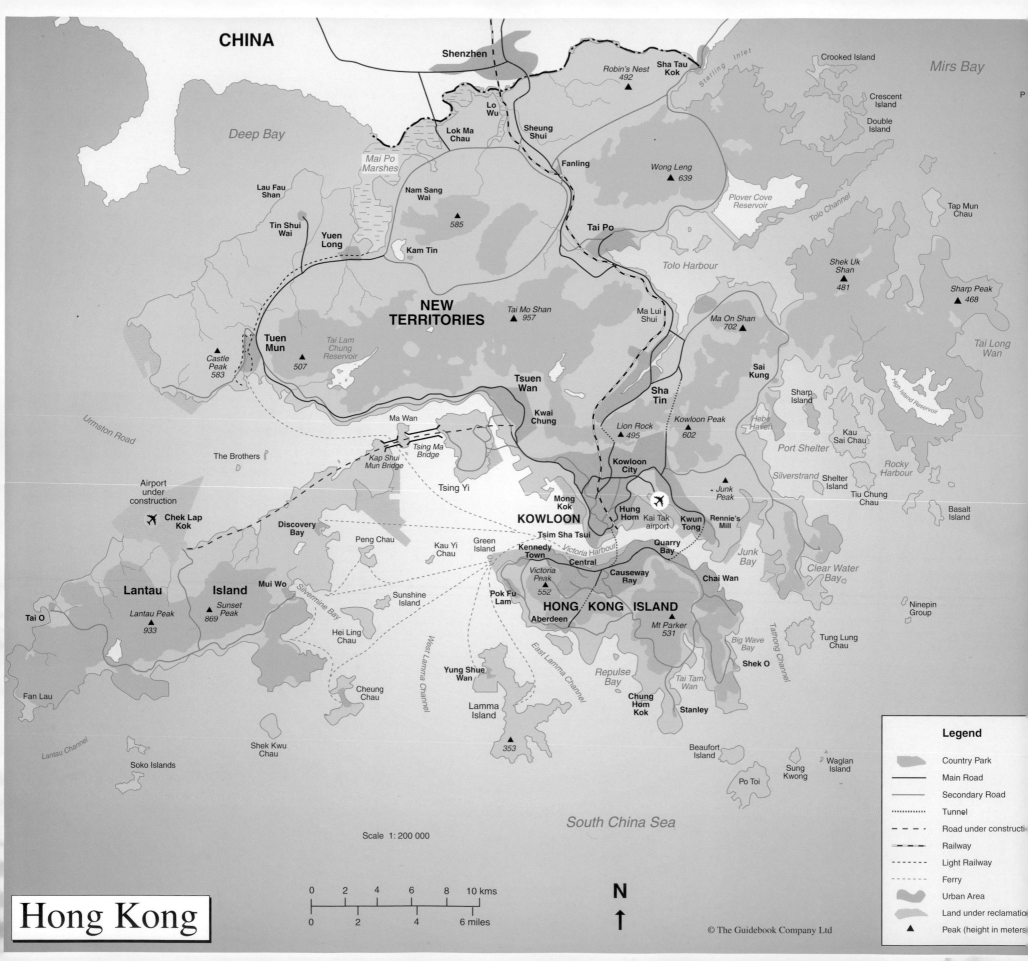

Hong Kong

CHINA

Shenzhen

Robin's Nest
492 ▲
Sha Tau Kok

Mirs Bay

Crooked Island

Crescent Island

Double Island

Lo Wu

Starling Inlet

Lok Ma Chau
Sheung Shui

Deep Bay

Mai Po Marshes

Fanling

Wong Leng
▲ 639

Plover Cove Reservoir

Tap Mun Chau

Lau Fau Shan

Nam Sang Wai

Tai Po

Tin Shui Wai

▲ 585

Kam Tin

Tolo Channel

Shek Uk Shan
▲ 481

Yuen Long

Tai Mo Shan
▲ 957

Tolo Harbour

Ma Lui Shui

Sharp Peak
▲ 468

Castle Peak
583 ▲

Tuen Mun

▲ 507

NEW TERRITORIES

Tai Lam Chung Reservoir

Ma On Shan
702 ▲

Tai Long Wan

Sai Kung

Tsuen Wan

Sha Tin

High Island Reservoir

Urmston Road

Kwai Chung

Lion Rock
▲ 495

Kowloon Peak
▲ 602

Hebe Haven

Sharp Island

Kau Sai Chau

Port Shelter

Ma Wan

Tsing Ma Bridge

The Brothers

Kap Shui Mun Bridge

Tsing Yi

Kowloon City

Silverstrand

Rocky Harbour

Shelter Island

Tiu Chung Chau

Airport under construction

✈ Chek Lap Kok

Mong Kok

KOWLOON

Hung Hom

✈ Kai Tak airport

Kwun Tong

Junk Peak ▲

Rennie's Mill

Basalt Island

Discovery Bay

Peng Chau

Kau Yi Chau

Green Island

Tsim Sha Tsui

Victoria Harbour

Quarry Bay

Junk Bay

Clear Water Bay

Kennedy Town

Central

Causeway Bay

Chai Wan

Lantau
Island

Mui Wo

Silvermine Bay

Sunshine Island

Pok Fu Lam

Victoria Peak
▲ 552

Mt Parker
▲ 531

Big Wave Bay

Ninepin Group

Tung Lung Chau

Lantau Peak
▲ 933

Sunset Peak
869 ▲

Aberdeen

HONG KONG ISLAND

Tai O

Hei Ling Chau

West Lamma Channel

Yung Shue Wan

East Lamma Channel

Repulse Bay

Tai Tam Wan

Shek O

Tathong Channel

Fan Lau

Lantau Channel

Cheung Chau

Lamma Island

▲ 353

Chung Hom Kok

Stanley

Beaufort Island

Waglan Island

Shek Kwu Chau

Soko Islands

Po Toi

Sung Kwong

South China Sea

Scale 1:200 000

| 0 | 2 | 4 | 6 | 8 | 10 kms |

| 0 | 2 | 4 | 6 miles |

N ↑

© The Guidebook Company Ltd

Legend

	Country Park
──	Main Road
──	Secondary Road
··········	Tunnel
─ ─ ─	Road under construction
─·─·─	Railway
- - - -	Light Railway
-------	Ferry
	Urban Area
	Land under reclamation
▲	Peak (height in meters)